# People Connectors:

## Elevating Communication for Educators

Terry

# People Connectors:

## Elevating Communication for Educators

## Terry L. Sumerlin

People Connectors:
Elevating Communication for Educators
©Terry L. Sumerlin, 2021

Published by:
S E Publishing
P.O. Box 796601
Dallas, TX 75379

ISBN:
print: 978-0-9659662-8-3
ebook: 978-0-9659662-9-0

Editor: Lillie Ammann
Layout: Jan McClintock
Cover Artist: Aundrea Hernandez
Cover Photo: Shutterstock/Jacob Lund

# TABLE OF CONTENTS

# DEDICATION

To all overworked, underpaid, underappreciated educators who matter so much. And to my devoted wife, Sherry, who gives so much time and talent to tutoring and to the Texas Retired Teachers Association.

# The Valued Educator

One who creates many ah-ha moments.

One who draws compassion from each student's backstory.

One who has confidence without arrogance.

One who is creative yet practical.

One who is in control but not controlling.

One who can handle discouragement without giving up.

One who sees success in little changes and small improvements.

One who doesn't know everything but knows enough to be an expert.

One who keeps learning in order to keep sharing.

One who's passionate enough to overcome obstacles of the profession.

One who "gets through" rather than "gives out" information.

One who smiles on good days and bad.

One who never loses sight of the objective and the mission.

One who laughs in order to last.

by Terry L. Sumerlin

# PREFACE

I'm a teacher, as is my wife, Sherry. Though she retired as a math teacher for a large Texas high school, she still tutors students and is active (as am I) in the Texas Retired Teachers Association. I'm also a retired teacher. I subbed one day for a middle school and immediately retired!

However, I still teach! Just in a different classroom. I'm a motivational teacher. For thirty years, I've traveled the country and written books in an effort to teach *People Connectors*—communication—to those in education as well as in other professions.

Whether teaching virtually or onsite, I'm often reminded of certain commonalities between Sherry's classroom approach to teaching (as well as that of other wonderful educators) and my approach at conferences. For instance, we are both passionate about what we do. And our passion has propelled all of us past numerous obstacles, especially those of the pandemic and the resultant virtual communication. We understand how draining it can be to solely provide all the enthusiasm that goes with virtual. We also know that it leaves a gap that begs filling. I provide the bridge.

No doubt, teaching in any form, anywhere, under any circumstances, has its ups and downs—as does life.

One of the greatest teacher ups is the ah-ha moment. The moment when you see the light come on. When a student gets it. It's that special moment when you know you've made a difference!

Were it not for the ah-ha moment that an educator created years ago in my life, I would not be teaching today. When I attempted, fresh out of high school, to enroll in San Antonio College, I was told I could not do so without taking remedial reading. It turned out that I was functionally illiterate. A reading teacher at that community college changed my life forever. Through teaching me how to read effectively, she, as an educator, forever opened windows of knowledge and doors of opportunity.

Educators do that regularly! You do that! You connect through effective communication with students, fellow educators, parents, administrators, and associations. You create ah-ha moments. You change lives.

Any teacher can give out information. Educators connect. They take the steps necessary to communicate effectively, regardless of the circumstances. Connection has the power to create a love for learning and to change lives.

That's what my writing, as well as my speaking, is about. It's about the frustration and fulfillment, discouragement and courage, exhaustion and elation of an educator. It's about how to communicate, including to ourselves, during the ups and downs. It's about how educators bridge communication gaps to create more ah-ha moments.

My approach is storytelling, with plenty of practical, common-sense takeaway. In what you hold in your hands, I share with you the same hope-inspiring, communication message and tips that I've shared with thousands of educators from Bozeman to Dallas and Birmingham to Guam. This book is about helping you as an educator and as a person. It's about elevating communication through everything we think, say, and do. Everything!

I tell audiences over the country: My effort is not so much to inform as it is to gently kick us on the shin and remind us of things we already knew but have forgotten or neglected. Excuses *help* us to forget and neglect. Let's reverse this cycle. Here's to more ah-ha moments!

# ACKNOWLEDGMENT

I am so grateful to Russell Cook, the owner and founder of ONBRAND, for the many hours he has spent patiently handling my brand and website. His advice, suggestions, experience, and expertise have been invaluable. And he's a super son-in-law!

# Section One:

# COMMUNICATING A GROWTH MINDSET

We may or may not be what we think we are, but we
are definitely what we think.

*Accept to connect.*
*There's no other way.*

# THINK ACCEPTANCE

The mind is a fascinating thing, isn't it? Sometimes, no matter how hard we try, some things just don't stick in our memories; while other times, with no effort at all, a certain thing we hear or read remains stuck for years.

Some time ago, I read something to which I keep coming back. In *My Father, My President*, Dorothy "Doro" Bush Koch tells a story of her brother George W. Bush and his relationship with his twin daughters Barbara and Jenna.

As Ms. Koch recounts, George and Laura Bush had their challenges raising teenagers, as most parents do. (Of course, now Barbara and Jenna are grown and successful in their respective endeavors.) During these trying years, though, their father would tell them something so simple yet so powerful: "I love you. There's nothing you can do to make me stop loving you, so stop trying."

What a wonderful thing for kids to know: that their parents love and accept them unconditionally! How powerful would it be for us to know that about all our connections, that we are accepted by others—unconditionally?

This concept reminds me of a time in the mid-eighties when I was a trainer for a well-known public speaking/ people skills course. The old gentleman who trained me to be a trainer said, "Terry, to teach this course, you have to have a high level of acceptance." I understood what he was saying then, but not as I do now. He was saying that to be effective, I had to be able to connect with *everyone* in the room. And, without unconditional acceptance, that would be impossible.

Now, he was not saying that I had to approve of or endorse their personal lives, their values, or everything they might say or do during the sessions. The gentleman was simply saying that I had to accept and respect everyone as a person, despite our differences. That, dear reader, is the key to connecting with everyone. Especially those we are instructing or teaching. Without acceptance and respect, there can be no connection, thus little communication.

But let's take these thoughts a step further. Unless we put our acceptance in practice—give it hands and feet so to speak—it's only empty talk. Acceptance must express itself in our actions. Let's look at three important areas of action, as I relate them to a pair of special connections in my life.

*Authentic Communication.* Fred Rogers said: "We speak with more than our mouths. We listen with more than our ears." Authentic communication involves the *more than.* It involves being in the moment and caring about someone. This is what happens for me on Monday mornings. When possible, I take one of our two granddaughters to breakfast. It's a special time for connecting with teen Amelia and preteen Lola.

During these times, we play a communication game that both girls enjoy. We take turns asking the other a series of questions. It's a time of sharing—not discomfort or intimidation—and the one who is asked the question always has the option of not answering. We keep our phones put away to give each other our full attention. Respect and acceptance are at a peak as we come to know each other's likes, dislikes, feelings, opinions, and thoughts.

I use this to illustrate how easily we can connect with teens and people of all ages, backgrounds, cultures, and environments. It just takes time and acceptance, whatever approach we use—unconditional, nonjudgmental acceptance!

*Nonjudgmental responses.* Someone has said that, if you don't want to hear the answer, don't ask the question. As you might expect, considering our age differences, on occasion the granddaughters and I have taken different points of view. Sometimes I just listen and learn. Sometimes we exchange viewpoints.

We don't have to agree to remain connected, but we do have to remain nonjudgmental. A judgmental attitude says, "I'm right and you're wrong." The message it sends to others often ends communication and severs connections when, if we thought carefully, we would know that's not at all what we want. What we all want is to be understood, respected, and accepted.

*See the differences.* The third area of action for accepting others is to look for differences rather than difficulties. Of course, we should also look for commonalities. However, here, we're emphasizing differences.

We often forget that, because of background, culture, experiences, education, and a myriad of other circumstances, we are different. Because we forget this, we tend to reject others because we perceive them as simply trying to be difficult. Let me show you this concept in action.

After many years of marriage, Sherry has concluded that I do not know how to make a bed and will never learn how. This is obvious because every time we partner in the task, she winds up doing my side over. However, in this, she just accepts that I'm different in the bed-making department. Never has she once said, "You're just trying to be difficult." I've just never gotten it down as to the correct way to do it. So, Sherry just accepts me and thankfully tolerates my lack of bed-making skills. With many connections, including with students, we can choose to view the person as difficult, which will possibly result in disconnect, or we can accept them as different and remain connected.

**CONNECTOR TIP: Think accept before connect.**

*Remember that trust accounts can be overdrawn,*
*but never maxed out.*

# KEEP IT REAL

E arly that morning I was sitting at the counter in the coffee shop of the San Antonio Riverwalk Plaza Hotel, staring out the window and waiting for 6:30. That's when the Bill Miller Bar-B-Q Restaurant down the street, one of many in San Antonio, opened. Then I'd walk the couple of blocks to the restaurant for coffee, a breakfast taco, and a relaxing place to read. When we lived in San Antonio, eating at Bill Miller was one of our favorite traditions. However, before I ever got to Bill Miller, a story unfolded.

As I looked out the window at the beautiful landmark courthouse across the street from the hotel, I was engrossed in pleasant memories from forty-five years of having lived in the Alamo City. Suddenly I was brought back to the present. "Hi, Terry!" someone shouted. I turned around and shouted back, "Hey, Ron!" Ron flashed a big grin and continued his morning routine for opening the hotel restaurant that adjoined the coffee shop.

Ron and I had become friends the day before. The circumstances of that day were a bit unusual.

The day before, I had gone into his restaurant for breakfast. The server seemed a bit melancholy, so I decided I'd brighten her day. As I often do with servers in

9

restaurants, I asked her name. "Sabrina," she said. So, I immediately started calling her by name. Her mood began to change slightly, and we started chatting.

Shortly, Sabrina asked my name and began calling me by name as she kept the coffee coming. In a manner of speaking, we connected.

After breakfast and several cups of coffee, I went to the register to pay. Sabrina met me there. I paid for my meal, and we each said, "thank you." "Thank you, Terry." "Thank you, Sabrina."

As I walked away, I decided to say something else to Sabrina. So, I turned around and walked back to the register. "Sabrina," I said. "I'm in and out of restaurants all over the country, and I always try to get the server's name. However, they rarely ever ask my name. I want you to know how special it is that *you* asked." She smiled in appreciation.

An older gentleman was standing beside her at the register. He appeared to be the restaurant, as well as the coffee shop, owner. He smiled but didn't say anything.

Fast forward to the afternoon of the same day. I'm in the coffee shop. Suddenly, from the restaurant across the way, I heard a man say, "Hi, Terry!" I turned around and saw that it was the owner I had seen at breakfast. "Hi!" I said and turned back around. Shortly, I heard it again, "Hi, Terry!" That's weird, I thought. But I turned around and again said, "Hi!" Then it hit me—finally!

So, I got up and walked over to the counter of the adjoining restaurant. I stuck my hand out and asked, "What's *your* name?" "I was wondering if you were going to ask me that," he replied. He shook my hand and said, "My name's Ron." Thus, the background for Ron knowing my name the following day, and how it is that through the use of names I had made *two* new friends in one day.

You might think that the point of my story has to do with calling others by name. Names are extremely important, as I've just illustrated. However, let's look at a couple of teaching points to be made from this story.

First, though I'm not a mind reader, I have an idea that what Ron really wanted was not for me to know his name. Rather, he wanted to know if I was real. Authentic. Was I only interested in his server or was I interested in everyone? In a nutshell, I believe he wanted to know if I was a fake.

Someone has said: "The secret of success is sincerity. Once you can fake that, you've got it made." Well, perhaps, but not for long. Eventually, most people see through a fake.

Authenticity in every relationship matters—a lot! Zig Ziglar used to say, "People don't care how much you know until they know how much you care." I would add, "About everyone."

The second thing I would point out from our story is that, though Ron wanted to know if I walked the talk, he also wanted *me* to know that *he* mattered.

This reminds me of an illustration that often comes to mind. In 2006, Reese Witherspoon received an Oscar as best actress for her portrayal of June Carter Cash in the movie *Walk the Line*. As she stood at the mic, rather than saying all the inane things that others say at award ceremonies, she said something truly meaningful. She said that every time someone would ask June how she was doing, she always gave the same response: "I'm just trying to matter." Reese said, "Now I know what she meant."

Aren't we all just trying to matter? Young, old, male, female, rich, poor, and everyone in-between, don't we just want to matter? The key to great people skills and great relationships is the ability to help folks see that they *really* matter.

**CONNECTOR TIP: Be authentic and they will listen.**

*Discouragement is in how we think.*
*The cure is in what we do.*

# TAKE CHARGE OF DISCOURAGEMENT

Have you ever been discouraged? Have you ever known an educator that you thought might be discouraged?

Perhaps because educators don't generally share their personal problems with anyone and everyone, we sometimes think they never get discouraged. Not true.

Everyone gets down from time to time. This is evidenced by the question asked by Chick-fil-A founder, S. Truett Cathy: "How do you identify someone who needs encouragement?" His answer, "That person is breathing."

Stated conversely, every living, breathing person occasionally gets discouraged. And we get discouraged for similar reasons.

We get down about personal finances, the economy, failure, rejection, family struggles, careers, relationships, health concerns, or a myriad of other issues. Educators are often discouraged because they're overburdened or feel like they are not being effective.

During these times, an encouraging word often helps. But we may or may not receive that word of encouragement. What else can help during these low periods?

Many find pen and paper (or electronic device) of great help during such times. Writing down all that is troubling us can be of great benefit.

Though imagination can often work for us, when we're discouraged it generally doesn't work to our good at all. Rather, it tends to magnify existing issues and breed new ones. However, when issues are in black and white, this is less likely to happen. And, seen in concrete form, worries often become less daunting.

Another tool for handling discouragement is to do something constructive. Personally, I've found that rather than remain discouraged on those occasions when a speaking engagement I really want doesn't happen, the best thing I can do is get on the phone and find a new client.

Whatever it might be that has us discouraged, the key is to not sit around waiting for circumstances to change. If possible, do something to change them. But, regardless, don't just sit and brood.

In close connection with doing something is doing something with others. Discouragement tends to cause brooding, which in turn hatches isolation. Big mistake.

People are sources of encouragement and opportunity. We can receive neither if we withdraw. Nor can others make us laugh, give us new ideas, or inspire us if we avoid them. In good times and bad, people are invaluable assets.

We must remember, however, that people are not to be used simply as whine bottles (i.e., to be used only for whines). Though friends can be good listeners during times of discouragement, they can also be a means of continuing to pour the whine, while prolonging our discouragement and making more of the situation than it really is.

And then, something we tend to forget in dealing with discouragement: As Abraham Lincoln often said, "This too shall pass." Life and moods tend to cycle. What is a really big deal today may not be so big tomorrow, days from now, or a year from now.

We've all heard that without valleys there would be no mountains, or that all sunshine makes a desert. Though trite expressions, both are nonetheless true. They also illustrate a principle that can help us respond appropriately to discouragement: we can't have the exhilarating, enjoyable times in life without having some of the other times.

**CONNECTOR TIP: Be proactive when discouraged.**

*Connecting is in what we say.*
*It's also in what we don't say.*

# CONTROL ANGER

Have you ever been angry? That's a little like asking if you've ever drawn a breath, isn't it? We've all been angry and likely will be again. That's okay!

Anger is simply an emotion, as are fear, sadness, joy, surprise, frustration, and many other states of mind. Because anger is an emotion, it would be foolish for me to tell you that we should eliminate anger from our lives. In fact, there are times when we *should* be angry. Such times would be when insensitivity, injustice, unkindness, rudeness, or disrespect is present. Anger, per se, is not a problem. How we channel our anger is a different matter.

As you're perhaps aware, I do presentations on *People Connectors*. However, there are also "disconnectors." I speak on those too. The most powerful disconnector I know of is uncontrolled anger. I know this from sad experience, and perhaps you do as well.

Oftentimes, the first thing we want to say or do when we're angry is the worst possible thing. We've all heard about counting to ten, right? Though perhaps trite, it's actually great advice. Delay is a very good approach when anger is involved. Count to a hundred if necessary!

Too often we succumb to what we think is an urgent need for immediate action. We go into motion.

Then later, if not immediately, we regret what we've said or done. The result is relationship disconnect—sometimes permanently. So, let's look at some important things to keep in mind when we or others are angry.

Aristotle said, "Anyone can be angry. That is easy. But to be angry with the right person, to the right degree, at the right time, for the right purpose, and in the right way—that is not easy." That's a powerful statement! It brings to mind two very important warnings.

First, be careful about being angry with the *wrong person.* We sometimes let anger simmer until it boils over on an innocent bystander. Then this person is impulsively viewed as a convenient or vulnerable target for venting anger in the form of rudeness or verbal abuse. This bystander might be our coworker, a student, our spouse, our child, our friend, or a total stranger. Though our provocation, frustration, or bad day isn't their fault, they become the cat that we kick, as opposed to our dealing with the situation or confronting the person(s) who really triggered the anger.

Second, we need to be careful about our *motives.* Is our anger for the right reason? Are pride and ego fueling it? This can be evident in the relating of events: "I set him/her straight in no uncertain terms!" In such instances, though ego gets a boost, maturity and relationships take a hit.

To Aristotle's wisdom, we would add that of C.S. Lewis. He addressed the need for *accepting responsibility* regarding how we channel our anger. He said: "It is only our bad temper that we put down to being tired or worried or hungry; we put our good temper down to ourselves." Most of us have been guilty of this form of excuse making. Instead of just taking responsibility for our bad temper and its manifestations, sometimes we just excuse them. Then we wind up repeating our actions in the future, while excusing them just as we did in the past. A better choice would be to simply apologize and state our resolve to stop doing what we're doing—no excuses.

When we apply the preceding concepts, in addition to avoiding relationship disconnect, we will be better prepared to help others when they are angry. Here are some simple, though not necessarily easy, steps we might take to help them: (1) Speak softly. (2) Ask questions that draw the angry person out as to the real cause of his/her anger. (3) Empathize, but don't beg the person to not be angry. If anything, that will make the situation worse. Instead, we might say, "Were I in your shoes, I would feel exactly the same way." (Were we that person, we would obviously feel as that person feels.) (4) Ask the person what would need to happen for them to feel better.

Some angry people we can help and some we can't. When we can't help, we need to be careful not to catch the angry person's unhappiness. In this connection a familiar quote comes to mind: "Never put the key to your happiness in someone else's pocket" (Chinmayananda Saraswati).

Whether it's a matter of our anger or that of another, if the relationship is important to us, we must keep that thought uppermost in our minds. Whatever gets in the way of that relationship cannot be good.

**CONNECTOR TIP: Check emotions before trying to teach.**

*Attitude is what we choose to take to or from others.*

# BE PROACTIVELY POSITIVE

What's a negative connection? According to *Terry's Unabridged Common-Sense Dictionary*, a negative connection is a person who is proficient in finding the cloud in every silver lining. It's that person we can always count on to deliver a good gully-washer on even the sunniest of days.

Do you have negative people in your life? Are you the negative person in someone else's life? One of life's greatest challenges is to stay up in a down world. However, there's a big difference between an occasional down mood (with the down interactions that go with it) and being a chronic grumbler, complainer, and naysayer.

As we know, such a negative connection can kill a home, a learning environment, or really any other environment! A negative attitude is contagious! So, what are the best ways to unplug these negative environments, *not the individuals*, in our lives? Here are three practical suggestions:

*Be compassionate.* You may be thinking: "Negative people drive me crazy! Sometimes I just wanna smack 'em (coworker, boss, spouse, child, friend). How can I smack 'em *compassionately*?" We've all had that temptation, I'm sure—but would such an extreme reaction help? Not likely.

Consider this: When a person is negative, it's NOT for NO reason. Is the reason justifiable? Who knows? But often negativity comes from someone who is unfulfilled, unhappy, or suffering in some way. They're generally not trying to be negative; they simply might not be putting forth the necessary effort to stay positive in a tough situation.

We would all do well to keep in mind the approach that Fred Rogers took when dealing with negative people. He would say, "But I wonder what was going on in that's person's day." We could add to that the words of author Mary Lou Kownacki, "There isn't anyone you couldn't love once you've heard their story."

*Don't take it personally.* There's an old line about the football fan who left the game early because every time one of the teams huddled, he thought they were talking about him. Though that's certainly a bit hypersensitive, perhaps the humor brings us back to a possibility we often ignore: if we are engaged in conversation with someone who is being negative—even if the negative comments are directed specifically at us—it is possible that the words are the result of "what was going on in that person's day (life)." They should not be internalized.

*Be the bigger person.* We know that certain diseases are contagious. If we weren't aware of that before, we certainly are now. However, what we are too often not aware of is that negative attitudes (as well as positive ones) are also contagious. Perhaps even more so! The difference between diseases and negative attitudes, though, is that we have total control over whether we catch contagious negativity. Our vulnerability or connection to negativity involves a few choices.

First, we can choose to be enthusiastic people, regardless. I know it's difficult, especially while in the midst of negativity, but it's not impossible. Author Dale Carnegie had the solution: "Act enthusiastic, and you will be enthusiastic." The moment a negative person starts to kill our enthusiasm, we're vulnerable to their attitude. So, we should act enthusiastic. We look them in the eye, smile, maintain open body language, and say something positive.

Secondly, we can choose to confront the negativity, carefully and compassionately. I like to take this approach with complainers: I sincerely express sympathy, and then I ask them what they think they might do about the situation. I resist assuming responsibility for their problem.

In confronting a highly agitated person, this alternate approach can be effective: Let the person vent. Then with understanding and compassion, call them by name and calmly say, "I understand. Do you feel like your reaction is helping the situation?"

With each approach, who is in control? Who's the bigger person? Whoever that person is, he or she controls the environment and the impact of that negative connection. Are these approaches effective 100 percent of the time? No. They are simply suggestions that can make us better people and better *People Connectors.*

**CONNECTOR TIP: Take positive action against negativity.**

*Look inward before outward.*

# START WITH SELF

It's amazing what differences we'll see in people from one day to the next. I learned a valuable lesson about this many years ago.

On that day, I arrived at the fitness center at 6 A.M., and only losers showed up. When I opened my business an hour later, it began a day of those who talked a lot and loudly. All day I had one interruption after another. When I got home, I had one irritation after another. It was an entire day of annoying people.

The next morning, though, was entirely different. I started the day with a nice breakfast at my favorite restaurant. Then, from the time I opened the door for business, I was privileged to serve many very kind, considerate, and thoughtful people.

What caused this change? Did the people or the circumstances suddenly change from one day to the next, or did I change? Obviously, my attitude changed. But what changed my attitude? I simply changed my actions, and my actions changed my attitude. That's the way it usually works.

This switch in attitude from one day brought to mind a story I'd read. I've always found it timely. Perhaps you will as well.

There was a grade-school boy named Johnny who was being quite a problem in class. Having already finished his work, he had loads of energy and nothing to do but disrupt others.

His teacher called him to her desk and gave him a special assignment. From a magazine on her desk, she tore off the front cover. On the cover was a map of the world. So, she tore the cover into pieces and created a type of puzzle. She then told Johnny to take the pieces back to his desk, to put the "world" back together and to be quiet for a while. In no time at all he completed the project and returned to her desk with the map properly laid out on his notebook.

The teacher couldn't believe he'd finished so quickly. "Johnny, how did you do that so fast?" she asked.

"Well," Johnny replied. "I saw that on the other side of the map is a picture of a man. So, I figured if I put the man back together, everything would be right with the world."

Isn't that usually the case? It wasn't the world that had a problem. I did!

**CONNECTOR TIP: Do frequent checkups from the neck up.**

*For best results, start with the best attitude.*

# JOIN THE "OPTIMIST CLUB"

I'm an optimist. In fact, we're so optimistic in our home we have snooze buttons on our smoke alarms.

You've probably heard of the guy that walked up to a Little League game and noticed on the scoreboard that one team was down 40-0. He commented to a player on the losing team, "You guys are taking quite a whipping today."

Without a bit of hesitation, the boy responded, "Yeah, but wait until we come to bat." In sharing *People Connectors*, I'm that kind of optimist.

Yet, I realize that for some, optimism seems corny and dumb. And, they may have good reason for feeling that way. It could be they've read or heard things about optimism that aren't so.

One of the impressions often left is that optimism is all that is required to accomplish most anything. Such is misleading and ultimately disillusioning.

A more realistic view might be to recognize that, though optimism doesn't of itself equip a person to do anything, it does give a person the mindset to do what he or she has the skill to do (such as teaching)—better than pessimism.

For instance, optimism alone won't make a person a surgeon. However, we certainly want a qualified surgeon with a can-do attitude. Few things could be more disturbing than to have a competent surgeon stand over you just before surgery and say, "I don't believe this is gonna work."

Similarly, in teaching, skilled, knowledgeable, and optimistic professionals are desired and needed. They are the ones who generally are most successful and respected. They also have less stress and experience less conflict.

Unfortunately, in some situations, not only is the teacher or instructor lacking in optimism, he or she discourages it on the part of students. Rene Descartes addressed this problem when he said: "It may be true that an optimist sees a light where there is none, but why must a pessimist always run to blow it out?"

It is self-defeating to take this approach. So, we wonder what would cause such. What's the cure? On this, I'll simply say one thing.

It could be that our fascination with the media (including social media) is one of the major causes. Understand, this is not a criticism of the media per se. It has a legitimate role. However, news can give us a distorted, negative view of the whole world and ourselves. This is due to the fact that unless something is the exception, it's generally not news. And those things that are the exception are often negative. Recognizing and properly dealing with this alone might improve our perspective, as well as our relationship with those we're teaching.

**CONNECTOR TIP: Be upbeat. It promotes learning.**

*"Cool" attracts. Drama repels.*

# LIMIT STRESS

It was a quiet morning, a perfect time for sitting down to write. So, with what I thought were fresh, timely ideas regarding stress, I settled in at the computer to get to work!

I began with a simple question: "Have you had any stress this past year?" After about two futile hours of trying to put together something on the screen that made sense of the ideas in my head, my question became much more than rhetorical. I was ready to scream, "Yes, I have stress! Right now!" The words simply refused to fit together, and I was totally frustrated.

Sitting at my desk, I recalled reading years ago that Agatha Christie bemoaned the same type of constant weariness from trying to put words in the right order, and she managed to write sixty-six novels! However, that bit of trivia didn't provide much encouragement for the moment.

Fortunately, Sherry suggested that it was time for us to take our daily walk around the neighborhood and thus gave me a much-needed mental break. So, after our walk, lunch, and some rest, I felt completely refreshed. Sitting down again, my thoughts finally came together, and in a few more hours I had the first draft. "Wow, this is pretty good stuff after all," I thought. So, I logged off feeling satisfied with the day's work, a feeling that lasted until I realized with a start that I had not saved the article before logging off. It was gone!

Later, the irony of the "stress" topic and what had happened would dawn on me. And after the sense of irony came, the laughter came—some time after, but it did come, eventually.

Immediately, though, I was able to start applying some of the stress-reducing tips which I remembered from what I'd lost. My first tip for reducing stress was most timely for me and perhaps for you, also, in teaching.

*Understand the real cause of stress. Real* is the operative word here. What is *real reality* and what we think is reality often get distorted by our imagination. As we know, the human mind is wonderfully creative. But the same imaginative power behind innovation and advancement can have a negative side when imagination makes reality appear bigger, uglier, and hairier than it really is. As a result, we stress. So, if we want to reduce stress, we need to focus on the plain reality rather than the version that our imagination has embellished.

*Don't Buy the Package.* In addition to creating needless stress, our imagination also tends to compound that stress into a *package deal* that includes a problem and the *presumed* reaction. And, when we buy the entire package, we stress even more. My writing mishap is a perfect illustration of this concept. The reality was that my writing was gone, except for what I could remember of it. The package deal, on the other hand, contained the reality and the drama of an assumed reaction. This might be frustration, anger, discouragement, or the abandoning all together of what I had written.

However, I decided to separate the two items, reality and reaction, in the package. The reality was something I had bought—rather involuntarily—but indeed, I already owned it. The only item I had a choice about was my reaction to the reality. There was a time I would have bought the complete package. Instead, this time I stopped and thought about a rational and productive response. Perhaps I've grown a bit in that regard.

How about you? How much of the stress package do you usually buy? There is no denying that nowadays there are tough realities all about us. I would not dare to minimize these unfortunate circumstances. From health issues to heartache to loss of employment to loss of income to school challenges to uncertainty, the list goes on and on. It's not my place to tell anyone how to respond to these issues.

I do think, though, that the approaches I've described can lessen some daily stress, even including stress related to the unwelcome changes. Some changes we have accepted. With others we have adapted. Some changes are still exceedingly difficult to handle. But, how often in our lives are such changes made even more difficult as a result of our negative imagination and the package deal?

Consider this: The only thing in life over which we really have control is our attitude and it, in turn, controls our level of stress. It also dictates the type of impact, negative or positive, that we have on those about us. This leads us to our connector tip.

**CONNECTOR TIP: Choose "cool" over drama.**

*Use the same attitudes that connected to stay connected.*

# HEADS UP, CONNECTORS

I'm about ways we connect through our communication. However, for now let's look at ways that we can carelessly disconnect, and how to prevent that from happening. If we prevent disconnect, we can communicate, and if we can communicate, we're in a position to teach.

First, consider this. There might be rare instances in which, for legitimate reasons, we actually *want* to disconnect from someone. It might involve negative circumstances, differences in direction, personality differences, or differing values. These things happen and, as a result, necessitate personal and often painful decisions. In such instances, let's keep the following in mind: (1) Try to disconnect without causing the other person to lose face, and (2) disconnect in such a way as to avoid regrets over how we handled it.

Though sometimes necessary, the decision to disconnect cannot be taken lightly. Keeping that in mind, and because generally we do not wish to disconnect from anyone, let's look at the mindset we need for staying connected. Heads up!

*Thankfulness counts.* Relationships generally have their roots in what we like about people. So, on this basis teaching begins, and all is well. Then, if not careful,

39

we begin to see characteristics that bug us. Also, over time, we forget the likes and the reasons the relationship was formed in the first place. And, in our minds, the dislikes become greater than the likes.

Though it's possible that a change in the other person has taken place, often the negative was there to start with, and we simply need to stop to remind ourselves of what the person has meant and does mean to us. Why did we connect and what would a disconnect ultimately look like? It could be that rethinking the situation will give us needed cause for humility and thankfulness.

*Introspection is key.* When I was in the high school band, my mom told me about a fictitious mom who was watching Johnny marching in the band at a football game. Suddenly the mom hollered to everyone nearby, "Would you look at that? Everyone's out of step but my Johnny!"

Well, that's certainly a unique perspective. It's also a perspective we can have of ourselves. It's easy to think that when connections become frayed it's everyone else's fault. But is it *always*? Perhaps, if I have a problem with everyone, *I'm* the problem.

With all of us and in all of our connections, we need to step back once in a while and ask ourselves who really is out of step.

*Kindness connects.* In his wonderful book, *Stop Talking, Start Communicating*, Geoffrey Tumlin says, "...kindness doesn't create a fraction of the problems that unkindness does." Ain't that the truth!

For some reason many in our society have decided they'd rather have the problems than be inconvenienced by applying kindness. Perhaps this is because of the prevalence of electronic communication, where it's so easy to be rude to those we don't see face to face and perhaps never will. Or maybe it's because, in the media, we see so much in-your-face communication that we think it's the norm and is acceptable. Regardless, one of the easiest ways I know of to "unconnect" is to be unkind. I like what Ralph Waldo Emerson said: "You cannot do a kindness too soon, for you never know how soon it will be too late." It's something to think about.

*Reason rules.* We all like to think that we are totally reasonable, all the time. I know I am. Aren't you? Think about this: Have you ever been angry? Have you ever been unreasonable while angry?

Not only do we tend to say unreasonable things while we're angry, we tend to say hurtful things. Often, when we're angry, the thing we most want to say is the worst possible thing to say under the circumstances. Someone, reportedly Groucho Marx, has wisely said, "Speak when you are angry, and you will make the best speech you will ever regret." It could be that what we will regret most is the loss of a connection that could have been teachable.

**CONNECTOR TIP: Heads up if you wish to stay connected.**

*Time is the essence of life and connections.*

# CLAIM YOUR TIME

**"I**'ll have my people contact your people." We often say that in jest, right? Have you ever wondered what it would be like to have "my people" who could not only handle some of your workload but could also take the pressure off by saying no for you? It would certainly relieve some of the awkwardness of saying no personally. It would also relieve the stress of overcommitment that is often caused when we just can't bring ourselves to say the two-letter word (or the equivalent)—NO.

In the workplace, gatekeepers and schedulers often perform this *no* function for others. However, even when such is done for an individual, it's not usually a matter of assuming *total* responsibility for that person's time. So, regardless of what someone may or may not be doing in our stead, there are still times when everyone struggles with overcommitting. So, how can we all say no when we should, and in a way that keeps us connected with others? As educators who never seem to have enough time, how can we gain better control of the time that is ours?

First, consider why we often fail to say no. I believe there might be one big reason. We're nice people. We don't want to offend someone or make them unhappy by rejecting their request or invitation. After all, if we make that person unhappy by saying no, then we might be made to feel unhappy as a result. So, we often avoid the risk and just say yes.

However, there's a flaw in this kind of thinking. Let's look at what can happen. For the sake of not making the other person unhappy, suppose we say yes to their request. We know that we don't have the time available and, not long after we commit, we *really know* that we don't have time. So, we wind up being stressed and unhappy because of our unwise commitment and lack of time. The other person is happy. Keeping them that way is why we said yes in the first place. But *we are unhappy*. Ultimately, all we've gained for ourselves is just a different brand of unhappiness—as well as stress! And our lives spin faster and faster as more things tend to fly apart.

Let's keep the following in mind when it comes to saying either yes or no to requests: If our happiness in life depends on another person being happy, we've set ourselves up to be unhappy (and overcommitted) most of the time. So, let's set aside considerations of whether the other person is going to be happy or unhappy with our decision and let's look at a few low risk ways to say no.

1. *Be polite.* We might make it a habit to begin our response with this or something similar: "Thank you for thinking of me (or including me). I'm honored." Then we can begin the next sentence with "unfortunately."

2. *Validate.* This is a judgment call as to whether or not this would be necessary in a given situation. After all, it is our time. So, it's not always necessary

that we give a reason for our decision. That said, after the polite statement we just mentioned, we might proceed by specifying why we cannot fit their request into our schedule.

3. *Provide an alternative.* If it's something that we choose to do, just not at that specific time, we might state when we think we will have time available. Or, if it's an urgent request, we might suggest that they ask for help from a specific person we'd recommend who would be able and willing to help.

4. *Either/or.* This approach can be used in more risky situations. Perhaps we're currently overwhelmed with a project, commitment, or responsibility. Then we're asked to take on more. In this situation we might explain our dilemma and then respectfully ask for input from the other person this way: "Which (project, commitment, responsibility) do you feel should receive priority in my schedule at this time?" We are not actually saying NO. That could be especially unwise in the workplace. We are saying, "Please help me figure this out." Will we get the response we're looking for? Maybe not. However, regardless of the other person's response, we've respectfully expressed our feelings.

5. *Delay.* We rarely regret what we do not say immediately. This is especially true when it comes to time commitments. Too often we commit simply because we say yes too quickly. Often, we should say, "Let me think about it." Then, should we ultimately decide to say no, we have had time to

think about how we are going to most appropriately express ourselves.

6. *Now rather than later.* The best plan in the world doesn't work until we do. The time for us to work toward making these techniques part of our thinking is now rather than when we discover we have to make a decision. Then it's usually too late and saying no will be as difficult and awkward as ever. So, let's review these concepts often.

**CONNECTOR TIP: Take action to control what's yours.**

# Section Two:

# COMMUNICATING
# POSITIVE MOTIVATION

For maximum effectiveness, the *why* must power the *what*.

*The best time for kindness is the present.*

# CONNECT WITH KINDNESS

A lady's voice came on the line. "Sometimes Cable. May I help you?"

"Yes. I am inquiring about internet service. I want to change my plan."

"I can help you."

"What I had in mind is a very specific kind of plan. The kind where I have service only about half the time. What would that cost?"

"Sir, we don't have that kind of plan."

"Sure, you do. That's what I've got now!"

I'm guessing I didn't make a connection that day. I'm also guessing I was not very kind and that I accomplished very little that was positive. Such is often the case when we're frustrated. It's also the case when various other negative emotions take over.

However, rather than using such emotions as excuses for unkindness, how about if we focus on what kindness looks like for educators and how it is communicated.

*Kindness is present active.* Let's pretend, just for a moment, that we are all unkind people. However, as a result of what I'm presently addressing, we all decide to be kind. By what number do you think the population of kind educators would be increased? That's easy to answer. Zero! That's because deciding and doing are not the same thing. Deciding is necessary prior to doing, but the two are much different. Being nice is not about what we plan to do, intend to do, might do, or could do. It's about what we do today. It's what we show to everyone today and every day, in every way.

*Kindness looks for the backstory.* Never will I forget Chris. When Sherry started the semester, she always told her students that if they would bring her a schedule of their extracurricular activities, she would attend at least one event. Chris took her very seriously. Not only did he bring her the schedule for his varsity basketball games, but he also made it a point on game days to remind her that he had a game. He wanted to know, "Are you going to be there?"

As I sat by my wife, I would watch Chris in the pregame warmups. He would look for Mrs. Sumerlin in the stands. Then he would make eye contact and nod, his way of thanking her for being there.

One day we were at a fast food restaurant when a very excited young man walked in. It was Chris. He had spotted Mrs. Sumerlin in the restaurant as he drove by and wanted to pop in to say hi. She had made a strong connection.

The backstory for Chris is that his mother was a single parent who never saw even one of his games. She worked to make ends meet. Sherry filled a backstory need.

*Kindness sacrifices willingly.* Kindness is not always easy. It requires selflessness. It's not what we have to do. It's what we want to do. My friend, Joe, illustrates that perfectly.

When folks run out of something to complain about, it seems that an easy target is the postal service. Joe reminded me of the importance of looking more closely at *individuals* in every workplace.

One day this past winter, after an ice and snowstorm, I walked into our postage-stamp-size post office in Lavon, Texas. It's so small you have to go outside to change your mind.

Behind the counter, as usual, was Joe. I asked him how he had weathered the recent ice storm. "Oh, I did okay. The drive across the icy Ray Hubbard Bridge was pretty tough, though. It took me an hour on ice to get here that morning."

"You came to work that day?" I exclaimed. "That's amazing!"

My friend's response: "I love my customers." He was there because he wanted to be. To him, the sacrifice was nothing. Whether kindness requires a big sacrifice or a small one depends on the situation. Regardless, it takes Joe's kind of selflessness.

So, what's our takeaway? What can an educator take away from these stories about a frustrated cable customer, a teacher, and a postal clerk?

**CONNECTOR TIP: On up days and down, choose to be kind. Nothing connects better.**

*People learn best when they see that we really want to teach.*

# SET THE TONE

One of my hobbies is a bit unusual. It takes the form of asking folks how they are doing and then collecting their answers. Some of them are funny, but all of them fascinate me.

Before sharing some of my collection, I wish to clarify something. I care about others and how they're doing. What I'm sharing is not an attempt to make fun of people. It's in order to make a point in perhaps a humorous way. That said, here are some answers that I've collected to the question, "How are you?"

"I can't complain."

It almost sounds as if the person is determined to suffer silently but wants everyone to know about it.

"Not too bad."

We're tempted to ask, "Well, how bad are you?"

"I'm tired."

Though this seems to be the required response of young people working in fast food restaurants, it's also the number one answer of thousands of Americans who were polled.

"Not bad under the circumstances."

This response sort of makes you wonder why a professional would be *under* the circumstances in the first place.

"Don't ask."

It's too late. I already have. But something tells me it was a mistake because I'm about to hear more than I planned on.

"I'm here."

This always reminds me of the story about the man who, back in the 70s, found a hippie in his closet. When asked what he was doing in there, the hippie replied, "Like man, ya' gotta be somewhere."

"So far, so good."

This is far from the optimism of the guy who fell from a ten-story window. As he passed each floor, he said, "So far, so good!"

"I am fine. Thank you for asking. How are you?"

This response is a breath of fresh air. Though often spoken by someone who, like all of us, could complain, is tired, and could easily be under the circumstances and pessimistic; they, on the other hand, while not misrepresenting their relative fineness, simply manifest a positive perspective and an upbeat attitude that inspires others as well as themselves.

Notice I said, "as well as themselves." No matter who asks the question, we are the ones most impacted by our answer! It sets our attitude and tone for the day. What we, as it were, whisper to others we shout to ourselves.

**CONNECTOR TIP: Project a positive attitude for learning.**

*When we make them thirsty, they drink.*

# MAKE THEM THIRSTY

I once owned a business across the street from a convenience store. Nearly every morning I would walk across the street to get coffee. One morning, as I was waiting in line at the register, the cashier scanned the purchases for the customer in front of me. When she came to his coffee, she entered the amount manually. Seeing the amount on the screen, he immediately reacted rather strongly.

"Naw! Take that off," he said. "I'm not about to pay that for a cup of coffee." The cashier, without so much as a change in expression, took off that item.

However, it's what happened next that is a commentary on human nature.

The customer asked for a few lottery tickets. Evidently, they weren't overpriced.

As the gentleman headed out the door, I stepped to the counter and smiled at the familiar face behind the register.

"Don't say a word," she said.

"You know what I'm thinking," I replied.

"Yeah, I know what you're thinking," she said with a smile. "Don't say it."

We laughed, and I left—without saying a word. But now I will.

First, a word about perceived value. When, as a boy, I would agonize over whether I ought to spend a certain amount of money on a certain item, Dad would say, "Son, it's worth whatever you're willing to pay for it."

Similarly, the difference in the value of a cup of coffee and of a lottery ticket (as well as many other things in life) is the difference in who's buying. Though it's none of my business whether someone buys a lottery ticket or not, personally, I wouldn't give two cents for one. On the other hand, I've been known to pay several bucks for coffee. People have different values.

Second, people are motivated by different things. I once read of a salesman who made no sales for the day. When questioned by his sales manager, his response was, "You know what they say. You can lead a horse to water, but you can't make him drink."

His manager wisely responded: "You have it all wrong. Your job isn't to make the horse drink. Your job is to make the horse thirsty."

The convenience store customer was thirsty for the lottery tickets because he saw the possibility of gain. To him, there was a strong WIIFM (What's In It For Me?). If the man could have been persuaded that buying the coffee would have satisfied a need stronger than mere physical appetite, I'm confident he would have been thirsty and the price would not have mattered. In my case, making me thirsty for a lottery ticket would be a very tough job.

Lastly, the incident brings to mind how people have different likes. I've often thought that if everyone had the same likes, every man would want to be married to my wife.

From another perspective, maybe nobody would want to marry her.

For such reasons, the convenience store brews many different flavors of coffee to suit different tastes. They also have different products to suit different priorities and motivations. Educators benefit by keeping this in mind. It can make learners thirsty for what we have to offer.

**CONNECTOR TIP: Stress the WIIFM for your students.**

*Accept only those excuses from yourself that you would accept from others.*

# MAKE AN HONEST EFFORT

What's your excuse? What's mine? We all make them. Excuses are so convenient. They're so practical. They're so handy for anything we really don't want to do.

We even have an excuse for excuses: "It's the truth!" Somehow, we figure if we're not lying in what we tell ourselves or others, then the excuse is acceptable.

"Excuse," in its noun form, is "something offered as justification or as grounds for being excused" (*Merriam-Webster*). Though we can lie in making excuses, nowhere is lying inherent in the definition. However, inherent in excuses is the fact that while we're making them, we're not making much else—including connections.

Connections require effort in soft skills (people skills). And, since excuses stifle effort, they short circuit connections. Thus, communication is impeded, and teaching goes out the window. So, let's look at some common soft-skills excuses from which we would be wise to disconnect.

*It feels weird.* In the late 1970s I was introduced to a book that I should have heard about long before. It is *How to Win Friends and Influence People*, by Dale Carnegie. I would not be doing what I do today were it not for how that book changed my life. However, at first, I resisted application of the soft skills Carnegie taught. I noticed that more people did not apply the principles than did, and I didn't want to feel weird or different. Then it dawned on me. If I wanted my *life to be different*, and I really did, *I would have to be different*. I would just have to feel weird until my new skills felt natural. The same is true for everything that takes us out of our comfort zone.

*I don't have time for soft skills*. This excuse says that immediate results are all that matter. Just get it done. Thus, a person can say or do whatever it takes to achieve the objective quickly. But consider this. A German proverb says, "Do it once and do it right, and you don't have to do it again." If you don't have time to do it right in the use of soft skills to start with, what makes you think there will be time to have the conversation again to repair the resultant relational damage? Treating others with respect is never a waste of time. It's an investment.

*Soft skills won't work*. Work is the operative word here. Work in what way? Too often, as previously indicated, immediate results are the objective, and manipulation or browbeating are the tools that are used to get it done quickly. However, relational damage, resentment, and failure are too often the consequences. Soft skills, on the other hand, are documented as achieving better results in communicating ideas.

*I plan to work on my soft skills*. Perhaps you've heard about the five frogs that are sitting on a log. Four decide to jump off. How many are left? Five. That's because there's a big difference between deciding (planning) and doing. Of all the excuses we could offer for ignoring or neglecting soft skills, this is the most insidious. With it we get the conscience comfort that comes from counterfeit commitment. However, even though doing is the result of deciding, commitment is always in the doing. Not the deciding.

I do not wish to leave the impression that we are all totally lacking in soft skills. I don't believe that of any of us. On the other hand, we often get lax in our effort.

My point is the same as what I tell audiences all over the country. My job is not so much to inform as it is to gently kick us on the shin and remind us of things we already knew but have forgotten or neglected. Excuses help us to forget and neglect. Let's reverse this cycle.

**CONNECTOR TIP: Make an effort, not an excuse.**

# Section Three:

# COMMUNICATING PROFESSIONALISM

Everything we do or say, in every way, every day,
throughout the day, intentionally and unintentionally,
sends a positive or negative message to others.

*Learning is a sure sign that someone got through to someone else.*

# GET THE FACTS

One of my favorite writers, Sydney J. Harris, was a longtime columnist for the *Chicago Daily News*. Known for his penetrating and thought-provoking comments on people and life, he said this: "Information is giving out; communication is getting through."

Are we getting through? If not, why not? I'm not smart enough to know all the reasons. However, from personal experience as well as observation, I've concluded that too much communication fails for one major reason: we have bought into certain myths regarding the process. Let's examine four of them.

*Myth #1—We communicate when we talk.* Though we generally communicate when we talk, we often make erroneous assumptions about talking. First, we assume that talking is the only means of communication. It's not (we'll cover that in Myth #2). We also tend to make an erroneous assumption about the communication process. We assume that all talking is communicating. Consider this: We communicate successfully when the other person receives the message we intended to convey. Conversely, we communicate unsuccessfully (we fail to communicate) when they don't receive that message, regardless of the message we intended. At such times, we talk but *we don't communicate.*

Unfortunately, many put all the emphasis on the message sent rather than on the all-important message received. Again, communication is getting through.

*Myth #2—We can choose to not communicate.* It is true that we can stop using words, if that is what we mean by "not communicate." It is not true that we are able to *not* communicate. Words are only one form of communication. The most powerful form is body language. In fact, body language provides an excellent clue as to why we often fail with words. It's because our words are saying one thing while our body language is saying something else. For example, I may claim to be happy. But if I forget to tell my face, the message received is, "Terry's not happy." Similarly, a person may say, "I just don't have anything to say." However, body language might say that there is more going on than is admitted.

In light of such, we must guard against sending messages of anger, boredom, insecurity, frustration, or nervousness during those times when we're unaware that we're communicating anything at all. *We're always communicating.*

*Myth #3—People skills don't matter in communication.* Think for a moment of a great communicator. Who comes to mind? It might be someone you know personally or maybe someone you don't know. It could be someone either living or deceased. Perhaps it's someone famous. Whoever that person is, think about what makes him or her a great communicator. Is it just the ability to put words together in speaking or writing? That's certainly a vital part of exceptional communication. People skills are also vital! If, as we've noted, communication is mostly about the message received and if no one wants to receive our message because of who we are, what difference does it make how well we deliver it?

Most great communicators, as well as educators, are the type of people that others want to listen to. They've earned that regard through great people skills.

*Myth #4—One size fits all in communication.* We're all familiar with the "fits all" concept in certain types of apparel. It generally means that the items thus produced are cheaper to make and therefore cheaper to buy. Communication is much different. One size does *not* fit all. Also, effective communication, unlike items that are mass produced, doesn't come cheaply. The price involves lots of personal effort, which also involves an individualized approach.

For instance, some people are introverts, and some are extroverts. Some are get-it-doners; some are get-it-righters. Some are leaders; some are followers. We're all different. We respond to different communication styles. Great communicators know this, and tailor their approach as much as possible. Poor communicators just say whatever pops into their head, and let the other person figure it out—or not. Afterwards the unsuccessful communicator is clueless in figuring out what went wrong. "All I said was..." The question is: what got through?

**CONNECTOR TIP: Look for ways to get through.**

*Communicate in a way that fits.*

# TAILOR COMMUNICATION

While batting, a player on our girls' softball team was hit on the hand by a pitch. The other coaches and I were concerned because the nine-year-old was in a lot of pain. Fortunately, it turned out to be a minor injury.

After she was replaced by another player and took a seat in the dugout, the girl was still sobbing. One of the first players to greet her was our eight-year-old granddaughter. Lola had a simple question for her injured teammate. "Are ya gonna die?" They both laughed and laughed, and that was the end of that. I wonder, though, what adult could have said the same thing, in the same way, to the same girl and gotten the same results. The relationship of the coaches to the injured player is much different from that of her teammates. Thus, what and how we would have communicated was much different.

This story illustrates something very important. It tells us that for communication to be effective, the content must be governed by the *subject*—the *what* by the *who*. Too often we're prone to just say what we want to say and then hope for a good outcome, rather than first giving thought to the person(s) to whom we're speaking and the circumstances.

We stand a much better chance, therefore, of communicating effectively (both in the room and with Zoom) if we keep in mind our relationship to the person and the words that are most suited to *that* person in *that* situation. Adult to child is one of many challenging communication situations where paying attention to the *who* is very important. Let's look at two other communication challenges where the *what* should be determined largely by the *who*.

Occasionally, we're involved in communication with someone who's angry. What might we do with this challenge?

First, keeping the attitude of the person in mind, we want to check our own emotions and be careful not to say (or do) anything that might inflame their anger. From this perspective, we would soften our voice, speak calmly, and begin by gently calling the person by name. Then we might proceed by simply acknowledging the anger in this (adaptable) fashion: "Suzie, I can see that this really upsets you. In your place I might feel the same way. Help me to clearly understand what you're thinking."

Note that at this stage we're not trying to reason with Suzie. This is because, while angry, a person is usually *unreasonable*. Reasoning at this point would be about like trying to reason with a person who's in love. Emotion is doing their reasoning for them. We're just trying to get Suzie to *be* reasonable so that reasoning might be possible. So, our communication approach would be to first calm her down through our own calmness. Then we're in a better position for reasoning.

Anger is closely related to a second communication challenge—confusion. Oftentimes, those who are confused get frustrated, then angry. We've all been there, right?

The good news is, as author Andy Andrews says, "Confusion precedes learning." It's a process. The bad news is that frustration often prevents us from seeing very far ahead. And anger prevents us from seeing at all. This might tell us something about why so many hate change. Often, what we really hate is the early transition or learning cycle that we remember from negative experience: confusion—frustration—anger. As I said, we've all been there.

From the perspective of having been there, how might we help someone who is confused or frustrated? What if we communicate with them in the same way as we would want another to communicate with us in a similar situation?

We would want patience and understanding, right? Both can be easily conveyed through personal stories. The stories might be prefaced with, "I've been there. I felt somewhat the same way when..." This is a way of telling the other person that we care, and that to some extent we know how he or she feels and that we understand.

Caution needs to be exercised here. Avoid saying that you understand if you can't or don't. Also, don't put too much stock in the exaggerations of a confused or frustrated person, especially if they're angry. Emotionally charged exaggerations are common and should *generally* be ignored and then forgotten. Instead, ask for specifics regarding areas of confusion or frustration and stick to a discussion of these. Then lead, inspire, and encourage with positive reinforcement.

There are many other challenging communication situations. I hope that the ones we've looked at make us more aware of various types as we communicate. More specifically, I hope that they will cause us to ask ourselves some much-needed questions every time before speaking. Who am I speaking to? What are their attitudes and circumstances?

**CONNECTOR TIP: Use communication specific to the recipient(s) and the circumstances.**

*Listening is transparent communication.
Through it, others see how much we care about
connecting.*

# LISTEN UP

There are devices that are designed to improve hearing. They're called hearing aids, and they've been available since 1913. As you know, modern hearing aids can be very expensive. They can also be highly ineffective when kept in a drawer instead of the ears. But, even when used properly, they only improve hearing, not listening!

However, there are such things as listening aids. They're highly effective and cost nothing but effort. Let's look at four of these aids that we too often keep in a drawer. They are vital to educators.

First there is the aid of undivided attention. I once knew a barber who would get so engrossed in what he was telling a customer that he would shut off his clippers, stop working, and stand in front of his customer where he would hold court. I wonder how the customer would have felt had the barber focused in the same manner on just listening to him. Not only is undivided attention a high compliment, undivided attention greatly reduces misunderstandings. Lack of attention, on the other hand, can be insulting and constitutes ineffective listening.

Second, let's think about listening in relation to proper use of the eyes. Studies have shown that confident people tend to look others in the eye for approximately seven seconds and then look away for about seven seconds before looking back. Looking away, however, doesn't mean a distracted type of looking about. Nor should we be looking at people as if to bore a hole through them. We should be looking as a means of listening. The eyes tell us many things that the ears do not. The ears don't pick up body language, gestures, facial expressions, and overall demeanor. Yet, they all affect understanding.

The third aid affecting how well we listen is the condition of the mind. Our auditory system doesn't work properly if there is a short circuit in the brain. Similarly, if our minds are closed, we don't listen well. The result can be what our spouses sometimes call selective listening. As an illustration, I hear baseball announcers on TV just fine. I tend not to hear Sherry very well, though, when she tells me something during a game. I also don't hear very well when I've already made up my mind on a matter.

The most important listening aid, though, is the heart. This reminds me of one of my favorite people of years past, Art Linkletter. He was such a great listener. I fondly remember, as a child, watching his *House Party* on TV and hearing his wonderful interviews of children.

One day, Art had an especially interesting conversation with a little boy. The conversation went somewhat in this manner:

"What is your name?" Art asked.

"Tommy."

"How old are you, Tommy?"

"Eight."

"What do you want to be when you grow up?"

"I want to be an airplane pilot," Tommy replied.

"Wow, that's great! Tommy, would you like to pretend right now that you are an airplane pilot?"

The boy smiled and nodded approval.

Art then said, "Okay. Let's pretend that you're flying a plane with two hundred passengers, across the ocean, and suddenly you realize your engines are no longer working. What are you going to do?"

After thinking for a moment, Tommy replied, "First, I would put on the fasten seat belt sign. *Then I would parachute out.*"

The studio audience roared with laughter. But Art never took his eyes off the little boy. When the laughter ended, Art looked into the tear-filled eyes of the little boy and asked, "Tommy, why would you parachute out?"

"To go get fuel, of course."

Art got the rest of the story because he cared enough to listen with his ears, eyes, and, most importantly, his heart. That kind of listening connects like nothing else.

**CONNECTOR TIP: Take these listening aids out of the drawer.**

*We listen with more than the ears. We also listen with the eyes.*

# "LISTEN" FOR BODY LANGUAGE

A young lady, dressed in business attire, enters a restaurant. Waiting to be seated, she leans slightly on the hostess stand as if it's been a long day. When she's seated, as per her request, it's at a table as far away from the other guests as possible. She orders, eats her dinner, and reads—without saying anything to anyone but her server. Well, that's not exactly true. To anyone who notices, though not verbally, she says a great deal. She's not rude. However, through body language, she says: "I'm tired. This is my down time and I want to be left alone to eat, read, and unwind."

This illustrates the first thing most of us need to know about body language. Every time we are in the presence of others, we are communicating by this very quiet method. It is unavoidable.

We tend to think that the easiest way to avoid saying the wrong thing is to just say nothing. There are times for all of us when that would certainly be an improvement! However, the *best* way to really avoid sending the wrong message is to always be conscious of what we say *and* do. Facial expressions, gestures, and posture send a message, apart from anything we might or might not verbalize.

This leads us to the second thing we need be aware of regarding body language. It can be, and often is, more powerful than words. In fact, when our words and body language convey conflicting messages, guess which message is received?

To answer that question, call to mind something you might have observed at a meeting or conference. The speaker tells you from the podium that he or she is excited to be your speaker. Yet, there's no smile, no eye contact, and no gestures. The speaker appears far from relaxed. Do you believe that they're excited? After all, that's what was said. But their actions say something different. Their actions say that they lack confidence or that they're scared to death.

Let's transfer that concept to communication both in and out of the learning environment. It's a nice thing to tell others that you appreciate them. However, they are more likely to believe your words if they see the smile on your face, the acceptance in your eyes, and the warmth in your posture.

This conflict between body language and words, and the power of the former over the later, is something that has been observed by animal trainers. They say that oftentimes the main reason some amateur trainers have little success in training pets is because the animal is confused by conflicting messages. The voice says one thing and the body language says something else. The animal instinctively ignores the words and obeys the body language. People of all ages often do the same thing. For that reason, we need to be sure that our body language always matches our verbal communication.

If it doesn't, our words are going to lose the battle between the two—every time.

The third thing we need to keep in mind is that since communication is a two-way street, we must always be monitoring the other person's body language as well as our own. For instance, if the other person tilts their head, it might mean he or she doesn't understand or doesn't agree. If they look at their watch, it might mean they're pressed for time. In that case, now might not be a good time to talk. For effective communication, we must listen *and* look for what is said, and then we must adapt accordingly.

Finally, we must not to jump to hasty, erroneous conclusions regarding the actions or mannerisms of others. Body language is best assessed contextually and as a total package, rather than when isolated.

By itself, the fact that the arms are crossed may not mean anything other than that the room is cold. It doesn't always mean a person is unapproachable or defensive. It might, but it also might not. Similarly, someone might wink because of a nervous tic rather than to flirt. Also, a person might raise their hand for reasons other than to ask a question. Common sense is always important to accurately determine what message someone is sending.

**CONNECTOR TIP: Look as well as listen for what is being said.**

*The subject has everything to do with the quality of our communication.*

# KNOW THE PURPOSE

I was asked if so-and-so is still alive. When I answered "yes" for the millionth time, the response was the same—for the millionth time: "Well, I'm surprised one of his ex-wives hasn't killed him by now." The fact that the fellow's daughter happens to be one of the exes might have biased him and stirred his emotions just a tad. However, I wondered why we must go through the same song and dance about my acquaintance every time he sees me.

I'd had enough! First of all, I don't care how many ex-wives my acquaintance has, nor is it any of my business. Also, and more importantly, I feel it is just as bad to listen to gossip as it is to tell it. So I decided to put a stop to it with a simple suggestion: "Why don't you give him a call and take that up with him?" It suddenly got very quiet.

We would all grant that gossip is not acceptable conduct. So let's consider some practical matters regarding the impact such talk has on character, credibility, organizational morale, and relationships.

Although, as we all know, you and I would *never* engage in this destructive form of speech, perhaps some gentle kick-on-the-shin reminders about gossip would be in order. Keep in mind, though, what Ronald B. Zeh said years ago: "The gossip of the future may not be a backbiting, nosy, tongue-wagging two-face, but a super-megabyte, random-access, digital interface." Gossip can be spoken or written.

The first thing we need to remember is what this form of speech says about one's character. Though we will grant that sometimes what we say about others is not as much a matter of character as it is carelessness, we need to give more thought to what we are about to say and then sometimes just not say it. It's so easy to drift from simple, innocent, harmless conversation about others into that which is harmful and should not be repeated, even if it's true. Some folks just talk too much and should be more careful about what they say.

On the other hand, deliberately telling or repeating that which we know to be harmful to another's reputation strongly suggests a character problem. This, by the way, is vastly different from saying what must be said about someone, saying it to the right person, and saying it for the right reasons. That's responsible action and requires courage. The other is irresponsible, abusive, and cowardly.

Another thing about gossip is what it does to the reputation of the one who makes it a habit. It makes that person someone who can't be trusted. It tells others that anything said to him or her, even in confidence, is not secure. It also says that if that person will gossip *to* you, the same person will gossip *about* you. As a result, trusting a gossip becomes a huge issue in relationships and organizations.

Gossip also indicates a lack of emotional and/or intellectual maturity. Those who are comfortable and secure with themselves don't feel the need to tell things about others that could tear them down. Rather, they are inclined to say things that build them up. From an educator's point of view, building up is part of earning the right to teach and of being a loyal colleague.

With regard to maturity and how it impacts what we talk about, it might be good for everyone to keep in mind what Socrates said: "Strong minds discuss ideas, average minds discuss events, weak minds discuss people."

**CONNECTOR TIP: Keep communication beneficial and uplifting.**

*Technology is best as a tool, not a crutch.*

# ZOOM IN AND MAKE CONNECTIONS

I was reading at an outside table at our local Starbucks when Rachel, one of the managers, started a casual conversation with me. "Whatcha readin'?," she asked, and we began to chat. I learned that she was in college and had ambitious plans for her future. I have no doubt that she will be successful. In addition to being bright and articulate, she's hardworking and has great people skills. But Rachel also confided to me that she knows there is one obstacle in her way on the path to her professional goals: fear of speaking in public. In this, Rachel is not alone.

I once heard an obviously bright contestant on *Jeopardy* tell Alex Trebek that, when he was in grade school, he was glad that his last name began with a Z, so that he always got called on last to give presentations. I got the impression watching him nervously recount this memory that he probably still liked to go last in that regard. I thought to myself, *Yep. Fear of speaking plays no favorites. Man, woman, young or old, very bright or less so, people of all backgrounds and abilities often fear speaking to groups.*

Why is this? I wish I knew all the causes. However, I do know some of the cures. I also know that more people are presenting these days—many of whom thought they never would—than ever before. The pandemic forced them to present virtually. As a result, Zoom (COABE for many educators) has become a household word, and though presentations have become more prevalent, they have also become even more challenging. What was once just a matter of simply presenting organized ideas to learners has now become presenting organized ideas *using technology*. Educators now have a much bigger ocean in which to swim.

I wonder: Is it possible that, in focusing on the technology required to present virtually, we have forgotten that presenting and *presenting effectively* are two entirely different things? What if a speaker botches the technology with what otherwise would have been a great presentation? Conversely, what if someone has a flawless technological presentation but lacks content or communication skills? In either case, the presenter will fail to connect.

It seems there is a need to go back to basics in presentation concepts, and then simply adapt them for virtual use. These are some of the same principles that I suggested to my Starbucks friend, Rachel. We all need to keep them in mind when presenting, especially virtually.

*Forget the nonsense.* As we were talking, Rachel immediately joked about the see-everyone-as-naked technique. Everyone's heard of it. The presenter just imagines all listeners as not wearing clothes. Supposedly, that way they seem less intimidating.

I'm reminded of a camping trip my wife and I took. We didn't want to be confronted by a bear, clothed or naked! Either way would be intimidating to say the least! The problem is not the group we're speaking to, but rather how a person views the presenting experience. It is the same fear factor whether the people are onsite or on a screen, and when you view it that way, it's about the experience and purpose—not the group itself.

*Speak to individuals.* Fear of speaking to groups can often be traced to viewing those present collectively. I mentioned to Rachel that she was communicating with me just fine. I urged her to present in the say way—directly to individuals in the group. Virtually, we need to do the same. Though we should look into the camera, the camera should be positioned so that we can also see individual's faces. We should communicate to them individually, as friends. That way, they become less intimidating as a group, and we become more effective as a presenter and connector.

*They're Pulling for You.* No reasonable group wants a presenter to fail. I asked Rachel if she had ever heard an awful presentation. Of course, she had. We all have, onsite and virtually. I asked her how she felt at the time. It's an awful feeling. It's awkward for everyone. So, whether we're novice presenters or professionals, onsite or virtual, those who are listening generally want us to do well and will, with certain exceptions, listen attentively if we prepare properly.

*Preparation is the Key.* Even though groups may initially be on our side, they have a way of disconnecting from a presenter who is wasting their time. Always remember, there are no substitutes for relevance, confidence, expertise, and passion. However, without preparation, all of these assets are wasted, as is everyone's time. On the other hand, when you as the presenter are well organized and ready to communicate the information, you will connect with your learners effectively.

**CONNECTOR TIP: Focus on connecting with people, whatever tool you're using.**

*The tools we use are only as effective as the user.*

# ADD TOUCH TO TECH

"**I**f you scream at me one more time, this deal is off!" So went the punch line to the story a friend told me about one of his employees. The employee kept getting e-mails regarding a business deal where the subject line was all in caps. So, the employee fired off the above response. The sender apparently didn't realize what upper case letters indicate.

While I don't recall ever sending someone that type of e-mail, I'm certain I've sent out my share of not-so-good ones. We all have, right? Yet, since technology is so much a part of our lives, we have generally learned what is appropriate and what is not.

However, like everything we learn, as we get busy, we tend to get neglectful. So, let me gently remind us of common-sense things about electronic communication (specifically e-mails) that perhaps we've forgotten or neglected.

*Give careful thought to the subject line.* Weird or mysterious subjects often denote junk mail. Thus, busy professionals, who do not recognize the sender, likely delete the message without finding out if it's legitimate.

The best approach is generally to, in a few words, state the nature of the message. Or if someone has suggested you contact the person, you might put that in the subject line. That way you get the addressee's attention.

*Be careful about forwards.* Professionals are busy. Because most get more than enough e-mails, they don't have time for or interest in cartoons, cute stories, or unsubstantiated reports. If you think you have something another might be interested in reading, it might be good to first send a brief message asking if he or she would like to receive the information in a forward.

If the person wants to receive it, send it to him or her without including the e-mail address as part of a carbon copy that includes your entire address book. Blind carbon copy (BCC) is a wonderful, professional option when sending the same e-mail to several at the same time. It protects each person's privacy.

*Use the addressee's name.* E-mails can often seem cold and hard. They can be softened by using the person's name. Depending on to whom you are writing and the reason, this is not always necessary. Nor should we feel we have to begin every sentence with the person's name. That's annoying even in conversation. But, when used a time or two in messages, the name is part of a high touch approach.

*Expect a response when the person gets to it.* When we depended on snail mail, we were more patient with the responses. Now, if the response isn't immediate, we want to fire off another e-mail. Thoughtful people avoid that. They exercise patience, and thus wait a reasonable length of time before sending a follow-up message.

*Never tell someone off in an e-mail.* Once you hit send, you can never unsay it. I know this from personal experience. It's a bitter lesson. Avoid telling off anyone in any circumstances if at all possible. Avoid telling anyone off in an e-mail like you would avoid a rattlesnake. Like the rattler, it will come back to bite you.

**CONNECTOR TIP: Whatever the form of communication, use it wisely.**

*All you can do is all you can do.*

# JUST DO YOUR BEST

Have you ever mentally beat yourself up over something you said or how you said it? Self-flagellation is generally as futile as sawing sawdust, but we do it anyway. *I can't believe I said that. That came out all wrong. I must have left them totally confused. They must have thought I was crazy. What an awful impression I made!* On and on it goes.

On the other hand, what if we handled it this way? *I wasn't at my best, so I'll just have to do better next time.*

As with many areas of life, changing a negative opinion of our own communication skills can often be a challenge. Also, even after we recognize improvement in how we communicate, sometimes a negative interaction makes us feel like we've reverted back to being a poor communicator. Perhaps the following A+ tips will help us assess our efforts fairly and feel more positive about how we communicate.

*Adjust your expectations.* Be reasonable with yourself. Someone has humorously said that a perfectionist is someone who takes pains and gives them to others. The sad part is that they also give pains to themselves in the form of unnecessary pressure and stress. This can be the case with what we expect of ourselves in daily communication. In this case, a paradigm shift is in order, one that recognizes the difference between excellence and perfection.

For example, if a golfer hits the ball off the tee, and the ball winds up three feet from the hole, that's excellent. If it goes in the hole, that's perfect. Realistically, even for the best golfer, how often does perfection happen?

Similarly, we cannot reasonably expect ourselves to be perfect in everything we say and do. We are human, and humans make mistakes. Moreover, there are many factors in communication over which we have no control—factors such as language barriers, difficult subject matter, or even the noise around us. We might also note that the standard for perfection in communication is subject to individual interpretation. What we might view as a poor showing on our part, the other person might view in an entirely different and positive way.

*Alert yourself to multiple contexts.* It's easy to forget that in every interaction, there are two (or more) participants who are communicating from their personal contexts. Each party's respective physical, mental, and emotional circumstances are involved at that moment. As our context affects how we express ourselves and listen to others, we must remember that the other person's context also affects how they receive and respond to what we have communicated. So, we need to cut ourselves and others some slack. We might get it right, but we'll seldom get it perfect—and that's okay.

*Avoid Avoidance.* Do you have connections (in or out of the classroom) with whom you try to avoid communicating because such efforts are always awkward or challenging? I guess we all do. Does avoidance ever improve this situation? On the contrary! This avoidance approach is not a real solution unless our goal is to disconnect from the person entirely. If we want or need to maintain that connection, we will find that a lack of interaction will only serve to worsen the communication that will inevitably occur.

It's highly unlikely that each interaction with a difficult person will be perfect. What if we were to simply settle for excellence (effectiveness) as the best possible outcome? Who knows? With that approach, we might eventually turn awkward into awesome.

*Acknowledge the role your ego plays.* One definition of self-consciousness is "uncomfortably conscious of oneself as an object of the observation of others" (*Merriam-Webster*). Egotism is defined as "an exaggerated sense of self-importance." Might there be a connection between the two terms?

There are times when we can give too much consideration to what others think of us. Author Olin Miller said, "You probably wouldn't worry about what people think of you if you could know how seldom they do." Though a bit cynical, there is truth in what Miller said. Ego goes on believing everyone thinks about us all the time. As a result, this "exaggerated sense of self-importance" makes us more self-conscious and less effective in communication. Then as a bonus, the ego tortures us with regrets after an imperfect interaction—long after your counterpart in the conversation has forgotten it.

By the way, the opposite approach to self-consciousness is also the product of ego. While self-consciousness allows us to be consumed by others' opinions, an I-don't-care-what-anyone-thinks approach gives no weight to anyone else's opinions at all. Both extreme attitudes cause problems in relating to others and create barriers to excellent communication.

**CONNECTOR TIP: Be kind to yourself when it comes to communication.**

# Section Four:

# COMMUNICATING AUTHENTICITY

Be the sincere person you want others to be.

*Have an ear for what you think others will hear.*

# PLAN FOR TACT

In 2013, my wife and I moved from San Antonio to the Dallas area to be near our family and, as an added plus, to have more convenient flight arrangements for my travel. Though Sherry and I were born in the Alamo City and lived there a total of forty-five years, two little granddaughters were a mighty strong incentive.

Not long after our move, our daughter, Amanda, had an interesting conversation with our oldest granddaughter who was seven at the time and thought that anyone over thirty was ancient. Amanda was talking about something we could all do as a family. "Wouldn't that be fun?" she asked little Amelia. "Grandma and Paca (yours truly) could go with us. We need to do that someday."

Amelia was interested but could see a problem with the "someday" part. She was also having a problem in tactfully expressing what the problem was. Finally, after stammering and stuttering a bit, she finally just blurted out, "By that time, Paca will be...!" Then she stuck her tongue out and slid it to the side of her mouth to indicate that by then I will have croaked. Such are the ways of kids. They just say it, sometimes with little or no tact.

"Tact" is defined as "a keen sense of what to do or say in order to maintain good relations with others or to avoid offense" (*Merriam-Webster Dictionary*). Children often lack that skill because of immaturity. It has to be developed.

Unfortunately, there are many who reach adulthood having still not developed tact. They sometimes manifest, as a result of less than tactful speech, a seven-year-old mind in an otherwise mature body. Thus, feelings are hurt and relationships botched as a result of needless offense. What might we do to prevent this from happening to our relationships, both professional and personal?

I would suggest that we, first, shift our focus from what we intend to say to what the other person will hear if we say it. Communication is perception. It is not so much what we say as it is what the recipient understands us to have said. Once we wrap our minds around that, then we are prepared for a three-way test.

1. How would we feel if the other person said to us, in exactly the same way, what we're about to say to them? Would we be offended or hurt?

2. Knowing what we do about the one we're talking to, how will they receive what we're about to say? What will be their perception? Will it enhance or will it injure our relationship, hence our ability to teach?

3. Assuming we're okay with the first two tests, do we still have any doubts about what we plan to say? When in doubt—don't. Rethink the matter. Is it necessary that we say anything at all? If so, it might be wise to give it more thought or to get some advice about how to say it tactfully.

**CONNECTOR TIP: Say to others as you would have others say to you.**

*Chew feedback before swallowing. It goes down easier.*

# DIGEST TOUGH FEEDBACK

It was in a former life, as we sometimes say. I was working for a large training corporation. I sat down to read the feedback forms from a program for which I was the trainer. One immediately got my attention: "It was a total waste of time and money."

I thought, *Shucks, if he had just not paid for it, then at the most the guy could only be fifty percent right. But that provided little consolation.*

I guess part of the pain at the time came from the fact that I thought I'd done a pretty good job. Also, I knew that I had worked *very* hard to deliver the best I had.

Perhaps you've had similar experiences. They happen to everyone, regardless of profession.

Virtual communication has changed or eliminated many things in our lives, but it sure hasn't eliminated negative feedback. Actually, experts says it's increased it. And regardless of how it's delivered, it smarts. As educators, we can't be important enough, good enough, or well-intentioned enough to avoid it. So, how can we more easily digest it?

*We must consider our emotional state at the time of the feedback.* Some time later, sitting in my office, I felt much different from how I felt when I first read the comment. I'd had time to rest up from the most demanding three weeks of my life, of which the program in question was second to last. Following the six-hour session, I was bone tired. So the criticism was viewed from that emotional perspective. General Douglas MacArthur said, "Fatigue makes cowards of us all." So does stress, insecurity, worry, fear, disappointment, and anxiety. All these emotions must be taken into account when receiving feedback or criticism, because any of them can affect how we receive it.

*We must consider the emotional state of the critic.* He or she, too, might be dealing with stress, insecurity, worry, etc. Or, as seems to be the case with the one who gave the harsh criticism, he might have an axe to grind. Though the person apparently needed *everything* in the communication program, as far as I could tell, he was not interested in *any* of it. Perhaps he was "volun-told" to be there. Yet, we've all heard that you get out of something what you put into it. For whatever reason, he or someone else put *only* money into it. So he got nothing out of it. Though we're not trying to judge him or anyone else, we are trying to be objective regarding all feedback. We always want to understand, if possible, the reason behind it.

*Focus on the content.* If as humorist Will Rogers said, he never met a person he didn't like, then obviously he never met some of the folks that you and I have. Some people are just not very likable, and these same people are even less likable when they give feedback. There is no reason a person giving his or her point of view has to be mean-spirited or hateful. But some critics are. In spite of that, we might still benefit from their input.

In my case, the strong words motivated me to give one of my best programs the very next day. I fine-tuned a few things, and I'm confident that had my "friend" been present, he would have thought it was at least not a *total* waste of time and money. So, our own attitude has more to do with the value of criticism than does the attitude (whether positive or negative) of the one giving it.

*Keep a good sense of humor.* Mark Twain said, "Against the assault of laughter, nothing can stand." That's why I started out as I did (in the second paragraph), and also why I sprinkled my thoughts throughout with a bit of humor. Humor saves the day and makes even the toughest feedback bearable.

**CONNECTOR TIP: Make feedback a positive part of growth.**

*Choose wise responses to foolish words.*

# BE TOUGH

I smile when I recall the conversation that I had with a friend years ago, when I lived in San Antonio. He's a dermatologist. In fact, he and his dad built one of the oldest, if not the oldest, dermatology practices in the city.

One day I casually commented to my friend, "I remember going to your dad one time when I was a teenager. It was when I started losing my hair." He thought it was funny when I added, "And as you can tell he didn't do me a bit of good!"

Today I laugh. At the time it was not funny. I was a fifteen-year-old boy going bald! Then I was a nine-teen-year-old, engaged to Sherry, an eighteen-year-old whose school friends asked her if I was her father. It was a very painful time in my life. Yet, as is often the case for each of us, pain was ultimately the vehicle through which valuable gifts entered my life. One gift was in the form of increased empathy for those who are hurting, whether physically or emotionally. Other gifts took the form of lessons learned about hurt feelings and how to deal with them. Though I'm still a work in progress here, as I suppose we all are, I take several approaches that help me a great deal. I hope these techniques will be of help to you as well in dealing with occasional hurt feelings in your workplace and elsewhere.

113

First, I try to put a positive spin on words and actions that might otherwise be hurtful. Of course, I'm not naïve enough to think that everyone, all the time, has positive motives. When I think back to teenagers who made fun of me when I was losing my hair, I'm certain they did not have positive intent. However, motive aside for the moment, who of us can say that we have not said or done something unintentionally that hurt another's feelings? That, alone, gives reason for being charitable toward others who hurt us. Perhaps they didn't mean to. For that reason, we shouldn't take it personally.

But let's come back to the thought concerning those who have *deliberately* said or done things that hurt us. In spite of how hurtful that person might have been, as we sometimes say, "It is what it is." So, what can be done about it?

Someone has wisely observed that suffering does not make a person special. How a person handles suffering does. Whether someone hurts our feelings intentionally or unintentionally, it is entirely possible that they will not give the incident a second thought. The question, then, becomes one of how much thought we will give it and how much space we will allow it to occupy in our minds. There are some instances, of course, when the person needs to be confronted. For the most part, though, we'd be better off to collect ourselves and to follow the advice of Eleanor Roosevelt, who said, "No one can make you feel inferior without your consent."

Another approach I've learned relates to something that author and motivational teacher Zig Ziglar popularized years ago. He often urged folks to "do a checkup from the neck up." During times—and we all have them—when I feel hurt and am playing the role of an event planner for a private pity party, I often remind myself to conduct a checkup. What were my thoughts and attitudes like before I got my feelings hurt? This is important to ask because sometimes, as a result of unrelated circumstances that have created a thin skin or a chip on the shoulder, we set ourselves up to get easily hurt. Perhaps at the time of the offense we felt tired, stressed, insecure, frustrated, or lonely. At these times remember this: people who are hurting are easily hurt by others. By the way, they also easily hurt others.

One other thing I would mention is in regard to personal values or convictions and how easily we can be offended or hurt by someone's careless words that hit our hot button. Specifically, I have in mind matters of political correctness.

As a speaker, as well as a caring person, I am very careful not to offend by what I say. Am I perfect? Well, ask my wife! Of course, I'm not perfect—nor is anyone else.

So, what's my point? There is definitely no excuse for anyone deliberately offending someone. However, there is abundant reason for excusing the words of good people who occasionally put their foot in their mouth regarding what is appropriate. If not, we're all in trouble. Therefore, if we're not careful in our assessment of the words of others, we can easily make thin skin and judgmental first cousins, while never recognizing the kinship.

**CONNECTOR TIP: Work at having a thick skin and a soft heart.**

*To disagree is inevitable.*
*To be disagreeable is a choice.*

# STAY CONNECTED

If two people are together for any length of time, they're going to disagree. It's not a matter of if. It's a matter of when. This should not surprise us.

These differences or disagreements are because we are different. Just as surely as we have different DNA, we have different tastes and draw different conclusions. And, when you add change to the mix, there are most definitely going to be some disagreements. Peter Shane, former Dean of the University of Pittsburgh Law School, said, "If you advocate change, you will have to understand that there is no change so small that it threatens no one."

Considering that we are all unique, and that we don't like change, we must learn to deal effectively and civilly with resultant disagreements—in society, in the home, with co-workers, and in teaching. May I offer a few suggestions?

First, recognize that just because two people disagree doesn't necessarily mean something sinister is involved. You might disagree with me because you're my friend, and you're trying to help me in some way. Certainly, disagreement might actually come from an enemy, just as someone who's paranoid might really have someone stalking him/her. But why must we assume it is always an enemy who disagrees? It might just as easily be a friend.

Second, when discussing a disagreement there are things we might want to keep in mind:

*Be sure to clearly understand* what the other person is saying. Unless you are able to state the other person's position in such a way that he or she would say "that is exactly correct," there is no legitimate basis for disagreement. In fact, it could be that when the matter is properly understood, everyone would find they are on the same page.

*Discuss differences with respect* for the other person. This involves avoiding cheap shots like, "I can't believe you said that" or "You, of all people, should know better than that." Disagreement is no cause for attacking the other person like a political opponent. Even if we think the other person's idea is the most off-the-wall thing we've ever heard, it impairs relationships and learning to say so. Always, let the other person save face.

*Remember that issues come and go*, but damaging statements remain. Though we can apologize, and often should, we can never unsay something. Be careful in a discussion when the adrenaline is pumping. If you lose it, you lose—every single time!

*Consider that we don't have to agree on everything* to accomplish great things together. "Two heads are better than one" doesn't mean "two identical heads." It means even differing viewpoints can increase brainpower and knowledge. When two heads always think just alike, one is expendable.

But what do I know? It could be we differ with respect to how to handle disagreements. You may take another approach. Is it effective?

**CONNECTOR TIP: Stay reasonable and agreeable.**

*An apology is a sign of strength, not weakness.*

# GIVE REAL APOLOGIES

I recently read where a fellow speaker said that he had a standard response when he received praise for a presentation he'd just given. First, he graciously thanks the person for the compliment. Then he asks, "What can I do to make the presentation better?"

I like that—a lot! Whatever we do, that approach has potential for making us better at it. Feedback is like that.

From time to time I get feedback from something I've written. It's often in the form of positive words, additional thoughts, or suggestions for various topics.

One reader recently suggested that I write about "how to say I'm sorry." The more I thought about it, the more complex the subject became. Like layers of an onion, there is more to the subject than just what appears on the surface. So, let's peel back the layers, while using a simple, four-question approach. It's an approach that could save an educator's credibility.

*What?* The Google definition of apology is "a regretful acknowledgment of an offense or failure." Generally, the acknowledgment takes the form of, "I'm sorry" or simply "I apologize." However, too often it takes the form of nonverbal, inadequate substitutes.

These substitutes might include, but are not limited to, showing special kindness, allowing time for the offense to blow over or pretending as if nothing happened. The problem, though, with such approaches is that they sidestep accountability and require that the offended person mentally supply the acknowledgment that is lacking. In other words, the offending party assumes that an apology will be read into his or her actions when there really is none, and they hope that the apology substitute will be accepted.

*How?* "Regretful" is a very important word in our definition. A person at a help desk might say "I'm sorry" simply as a matter of policy and training and have no regrets whatsoever. Or, conversely, in their tone of voice and manner of expression they might really convey that they regret what has happened and that they truly want to help. Sincerity is the most important part of an apology.

Brevity is also important. We should apologize in such a way as to quickly get in and out of the statement. Though we do not want to appear abrupt and insincere, we need to be aware that the longer we talk, the more likely we are to take back an "I'm sorry" by adding the word "but" or "however."

There might be a myriad of excuses a person will offer for improper words or actions. However, when it comes to apologizing for them, it's best to swallow all excuses rather than give them expression. Ben Franklin said, "Never ruin an apology with an excuse." The only qualifier that an apology should have is a statement of resolve to do better in the future—not a "however."

*When?* In what has previously been discussed, we've already noticed a good bit regarding when to apologize. Obviously, when we've offended or failed someone, especially when much is expected of us as examples. This is in contrast to the popular love-is-never-having-to-say-you're-sorry philosophy. I like much better the philosophy of Canadian cartoonist Lynn Johnston: "An apology is the superglue of life. It can repair just about anything."

On the other hand, we can get into the habit of apologizing too frequently. This involves calling attention to things that we say or do that no one notices or cares about. Some feel a need to apologize for such things anyway. This might proceed from low self-esteem. But what is often overlooked is that such apologies can exacerbate low self-esteem, as well as negatively affect the way others view us. So when to apologize requires good judgment.

*Who? Everyone* needs to apologize from time to time. I read of a CEO who contended that if he were to apologize when he made mistakes it would weaken his position in the organization by letting his followers know he made mistakes. The response was, "You don't think they already know you make mistakes?"

It's a sign of strength and courage, not weakness, when someone needs to apologize and does. On the other hand, it shows a need for growth when someone needs to apologize but won't. In that case the offended person has a decision to make, based upon the situation and the relationship. It could be that the offended person has an opportunity to make a positive difference in the other's person's life by being bigger than the issue and by setting a good example.

**CONNECTOR TIP: Be strong and apologize when needed.**

*Laugh as much as possible. Laughter connects like nothing else.*

# HAVE A SENSE OF HUMOR

Once, after a presentation in Las Vegas, I was asked how we develop a sense of humor. Because of what I'd said in the presentation, the lady seemed to realize that humor sells ideas, reduces stress, and builds relationships—at home and in the workplace. I could have added that when teaching, humor causes everyone to listen more to what we say next. In fact, attention is greater after laughter.

But how did I answer the lady about developing a sense of humor? Well, about like most who don't have a very good answer to a question. First, I said, "That's a good question." Then I gave a weak answer.

However, sometime after that event, I wished the inquirer could have been with me. Just by observation she might have gotten her answer.

It didn't start out as a red-letter day. Sherry was feeling bad because she had not gone to bed at all the night before. She had been preparing for the first day of class following the holidays. My widowed mom had been having severe pain in her lower abdomen for several days. A dear friend since boyhood was in the hospital across town with pneumonia. Several months prior he'd had a stroke. And, with all this on the back burner in my mind, my brand-new presentation that I was giving that night was on the front burner.

Though I truly wanted to check on my sick friend, I wasn't looking forward to the drive across San Antonio and the maze of traffic at the medical center. Refusing to be deterred from what I wanted and needed to do, I left the office and got in the car.

Before getting on the highway, I pulled into Walgreen's to get some breath mints for me and shampoo for Sherry. As I neared the cash register, I realized how it might look for me, with my smooth head, to be standing there buying shampoo. So, in order to beat the cashier to the punch, I smiled and quipped, "I picked up this volumizing shampoo. I sure hope this stuff works because, as you can see, I really need it."

The poor lady lost it. She was laughing so hard I thought I was going to have to ring up my own sale. When she gained her composure, she called a friend over so she could tell her what the crazy bald guy had said. They were still laughing as I walked out the door smiling.

The first thing I did when I saw my friend in the hospital was tell him what had happened at Walgreen's. The first thing he did when his wife later walked into his room was to have me retell the story to her. That night, after my speech, as I was chatting with folks, I told it again. Now I'm telling you.

Admittedly, the next stop with my story was not the comedy circuit. But that's okay. Just knowing I brightened a day for myself and others is sufficient. What made it possible? Simply taking my focus off self and looking outward at life, standing on its ear.

When I said "That's a good question" to the lady in Vegas, maybe I really followed it with a better answer than I thought. What I told her was that we develop a sense of humor by looking outward, and that self-centered, anxious people are rarely funny.

By the way, though Mom was hospitalized, Sherry, my friend, and my speech are no longer sources of concern. For the most part, as is often the case, I was anxious for nothing.

**CONNECTOR TIP: When possible, make them laugh. They'll listen better.**

# Section Five:

# COMMUNICATING RESPECT

To find respect, look again.

*Respect is the key that unlocks hearts and minds.*
*Let's control the offspring of our minds.*

# REIN IN PREJUDICE

It's fall at Terrell Wells Junior High School in San Antonio, Texas. The year is 1963.

President John F. Kennedy is the topic of conversation with students and teachers. He has just left San Antonio on his way to Dallas. Emotions are running high. Those who love him *really* love him. Those who don't—*really* don't.

During home room, students are casually milling around the room, chatting and waiting to go to afternoon classes. It seems like a good time for informal political discussions. This is especially a great idea since fourteen- and fifteen-year-olds know just about everything there is to know about politics—and everything else. The discussion heats up so much that one student decides to make his point in a dramatic, though very disrespectful, way. Because he grew up in an environment where JFK was intensely disliked, he disliked him. So with all the confidence and boldness that often goes with ignorance, he makes his move.

At the front of the classroom, high on the wall, hung a nice, framed picture of the president. The young student climbs on a chair and, with disdain for the president, dusts an eraser on the picture.

The teacher goes into orbit over what *I* did. He angrily says I will have to stay after school for such outrageous, disrespectful conduct.

A short time later, that same afternoon, an announcement is made over the school intercom. The president has been shot in Dallas. Later that afternoon, November 22, 1963, we receive another announcement. President John F. Kennedy is dead.

The teacher previously mentioned very quietly walked over to me and compassionately told me I did not have to stay after school. I guess he figured I was already suffering enough for my youthful stupidity.

This sad story is on my mind because at lunch recently our daughter, Amanda, asked if I remembered where I was and what I was doing when Kennedy was shot. I had never told her my story. Because our impressionable little granddaughters were with us in the restaurant, and because of the strongly divided political sentiments in our country, I felt it was a story that must be told.

I consider myself a humorist. I tell stories that make relevant points, while making people laugh. However, there is *nothing* funny about the story I just told. But there are important points to be drawn from it.

One point is that good people can be wrongly influenced. I was not a bad kid, and what I did was totally out of character for me. My parents were definitely not bad parents. They were great. We were just prejudiced. Why we were prejudice is not important. Type of prejudice is.

There is prejudice of the mind, and there is also prejudice of the heart. One involves preferences and things. The other involves people and character.

One type of prejudice can simply make us annoying in conversation with those who, for instance, like Ford products when we, on the other hand, have a strong bias toward Chevrolet. But it's otherwise harmless. The other type of prejudice *can* create hatred. It's contagious, dangerous, and often destructive. It can easily be taught to children and is often intensified through the reproduction of attitudes. And what's scary is that the process can occur in otherwise good people and families.

The second point of this story is with reference to something Benjamin Franklin said: "If passion drives you, let reason hold the reins." It's fine to take a position, whether in an election, in the workplace, in society, or in the home. It's fine to feel passionately about something. It's not fine to do or say something that is hateful or destructive or that you might later regret.

**CONNECTOR TIP: Check your heart before speaking or doing anything.**

*Value people over policy and procedures.*

# PUT PEOPLE FIRST

One of the many stories President Reagan liked to tell involved Communist Russia. He said that one of its citizens was finally able to save enough money to buy an automobile. So, he went to the proper bureau and filled out all the necessary papers for his purchase. Having done that, he was given a date of delivery that was five years away.

"Will that delivery be for the morning or afternoon?" the man asked.

The agent shot back, "What difference does it make? We're talking about something five years away."

"Because," the gentleman replied, "the plumber's already scheduled for that morning."

Reagan would use the illustration to point out the inefficiency of Russia's whole system. He would also, quite often, say that the number one job of a bureaucracy is to preserve the bureaucracy.

All of this came to mind when I was called on to give a speech to a government agency. I was specifically asked to deal with how to motivate those who are constantly coping with policies, paperwork, regulations, and red tape. Though a challenge to agencies, it's also the challenge of many in education. So how can we best cope?

First of all, since there is little choice, we can comply. However, in the process of complying we must also keep our priorities straight.

One of the things I tried to stress in the speech that I mentioned is that people are rarely highly motivated to serve bureaucracies. On the other hand, employees might have a better attitude toward tedious, boring, or stressful procedures if leaders impress on them that they're performing tasks required by certain agencies, without which the organization is not allowed to exist. And, by existing, an invaluable service is provided.

Looking at the matter from the other person's point of view, there is something else we can do in the midst of required procedures: we can shield them from as much of it as possible, and thus make it easier for them.

An example of failure to do that involves something that happened years ago in a hotel restaurant. I ordered a cheese Danish and received this reply from the waitress: "I'll see if we have one. Normally management doesn't like us to tell customers when we have them, because when we tell them we sell out too fast."

I thought I was hearing things or had just been beamed down from the Starship Enterprise. But it got even stranger.

The dear lady then went off in search of my priceless pastry, and in a few minutes came back to the table carrying my Danish on a saucer as if she bore the Hope Diamond. She had performed for me this grand service!

I still laugh every time I relate the ridiculous scenario in speeches. Yet, the sad part is that to management and employees of the restaurant the rationale behind their approach probably made perfect sense. The absurdity of it all, and how it epitomized slavery to a ridiculous system, was apparent only to others.

The incident itself didn't involve regulations from some sort of agency. However, it nonetheless illustrates an approach taken by many organizations, including those involving educators. It involves, above all things, strict adherence to systems, policies, and procedures rather than attention to the purpose for existing. As a result, enthusiasm is lost on the part of the teacher and the taught.

How do we do what has to be done, that perhaps no one enjoys doing, while enthusiastically doing what we are there for? Whatever else must be done, stay connected with the people and the purpose.

**CONNECTOR TIP: Respect people for what they are—essential.**

*We matter most to others
when others matter most to us.*

# DRESS FOR RESPECT

We often see businesses with signs that say, "No shoes, no shirt, no service."

Thankfully, there are still businesses who have customers for whom such a sign is not necessary. However, it seems that inappropriate dress is becoming increasingly prevalent, including in the workplace.

Sometimes I even wonder if underwear might have been misnamed. We would naturally think that the term refers to garments that are to be worn under other clothes. But it seems a growing number of folks think otherwise.

One morning, as Sherry was making her way to the school where she taught, we stopped off for coffee at a McDonald's. In walked a young man (likely a student where she taught) in his undershirt. That's undershirt. Not a T-shirt.

The teen walked up to the counter and asked to speak to his friend who worked in the back. When his friend appeared, he asked him if they were still hiring.

I don't know what he was told, but Sherry and I found it amusing (and pathetic) that he would even consider looking for a job dressed in such a manner. As it turned out, we had misjudged the situation.

As the young man left and went to his car, he began peeling off his undershirt. We immediately decided that perhaps he had dressed up for the occasion and was simply taking off his equivalent of appropriate attire.

Now, don't get me wrong. I'm not trying to be judgmental nor pose as the dress code officer. Actually, I tend to favor the approach of Mary Teresa Bara when she became CEO of General Motors. She reduced ten pages of dress code in the employee handbook to two words: "Dress appropriately." That places the responsibility on each individual.

But what does "dress appropriately" mean? First of all, it means the maturity to know and apply what is appropriate. Kids may not be there yet, but adults should be.

But what is appropriate? Basically, it involves observation and common sense. It's apparel that shows respect for the person(s) we are with and the occasion. It's easily recognizable and is respected by others. It connects!

What does this have to do with teaching? Simply this: people tend to listen to those they believe show them respect.

**CONNECTOR TIP: Dress to show respect and to be respected.**

*We can figure out many things.*
*People are not things.*

# KNOW THE KNOWABLE

It was 1997 and I was excited about doing a book signing for my first book. The event was in Corpus Christi, Texas. Though it was long ago, I'll never forget what happened.

I was comfortably seated in the Barnes and Noble and ready to roll, when in walked a rather attractive lady wearing a white jacket and pager. I was flattered when she immediately took an interest in my book and asked if I would inscribe it to her.

After I handed the book back to the lady, we chatted for a minute. Then she began to browse and to make her selections. Occasionally she would walk by my table, and we would chat some more.

At one point when she walked near me, I noticed that she had about a dozen books. I commented that she must really like to read. She simply responded that they were not all for her.

The lady must have spent an hour in the store looking at and collecting books. All the while, I was feeling pretty good over the idea that this well-read professional found my book suited to her discriminating taste.

Wrong! As my adoring public left the store, the manager was right behind her. My book, along with the others, was brought back into the store—to be sold.

I've often wondered how much they got for the book inscribed to my fan.

Following perhaps a chuckle, you might then wonder what this story has to do with teaching. Good question!

Actually, it has to do with all professions and inter-actions, especially teaching. It serves to remind us that we need to be careful about thinking we have someone totally figured out, whether it involves that which is positive or negative. We never do. Not totally. In fact, when we think we really know what someone will al-ways or never do, think or not think, be or not be, we need to mentally add "and sometimes they will; some-times they won't; sometimes they are; sometimes they're not." Otherwise, our approach will constantly frustrate us as well as sometimes/always/never help in teaching.

**CONNECTOR TIP: Expect the unexpected.
Assume nothing. You'll be happier.**

# OTHER BOOKS BY TERRY L. SUMERLIN

Available at Amazon.com

*Leadership: It Takes More Than a Great Haircut!*

*Christian Leadership: 50 Stories that Connect Faith and Everyday Life*

Also available for your favorite E-reader

# OTHER BOOKS BY TERRY L. SUMERLIN

Available at Amazon.com
*Leadership: It Takes More Than a Great Haircut!*
*Christian Leadership: 50 Stories that Connect Faith and
   Everyday Life*
Also available for your favorite E-reader

# BOOK TERRY L. SUMERLIN
# FOR YOUR NEXT EVENT

www.terrysumerlin.com
terry@terrysumerlin.com